AfO

Acting for Opera

A Manual on Acting for Opera Singers

By Norman Cooley

Heartfelt thanks and love to my friends Trish and Angela for their encouragement and particularly to my sister Candace for all her help and suggestions.

This book is dedicated all the teachers I have studied with and particularly two remarkable men, Mr. Rafael (Rudi) Shelly and Mr. Michael Gordon.

Table of Contents

i

Preface

When you think of performances in the opera house, how often do you look back and think to yourself, 'Sung well, really well sung. But the acting was so wooden, so clichéd, so awkward?' They sing wonderfully, they have a remarkable grip on the music and musicality of their roles. But the poor relation of Acting is the undeveloped skill and the elephant on the stage which everyone either ignores or just accepts is going to be there. Nothing to be done about that.

There are notable exceptions. The towering acting of Maria Callas comes to mind of course. And there are other famous singers of the past and some of the present who are clearly super actors.

But the acting standard in most opera performances I have seen is generally just about average if you are lucky. They rarely engage in the drama, the conflict, the relationships. The acting element of their performance, rather than meeting or exceeding the quality of their singing is generally 'phoned in' from miles away and they are just going through the motions. It's such a shame that there is so much emphasis on the singing and so little on the presentation. And there are many circumstances where if the singing is particularly good, then the acting can be really dreadful but it is accepted because the singing is of such a high standard. It's as if you are handed a 'Get out of Acting class' free card if you can sing exceptionally well. This applies particularly to voice parts which are rare and hard to find. Excellent lyric tenors. Very few. They are awarded the 'Get Out Free' card it seems from music college onwards. Their careers progress and their singing develops and they sing wonderfully but alas their acting remains in the doldrums and the audience and the critics just accept it. In many cases, the better you sing, the worse your acting is allowed to be.

There are reasons for this dynamic which are understandable. There are plenty of superb singers who are very average actors working in opera today but let's face it there are very few super actors who are only very average singers in opera. The audience comes to the opera to hear and witness fine singing. Clearly the singing should come first and should be superb for the paying audience but must we be complacent and not also expect good and perhaps even excellent complementary and integrated acting skills as well?

A common acting 'syndrome' opera audiences are sadly used to is no contact between the characters, sometimes called 'Park and Bark'. The singer stands and sings their role and that is all the audience gets. They have no relationships to the other characters, they have no contact with the other characters. The problem is if the singer is not involved, the audience will follow suit. This is dead opera.

Most opera singers have no idea what to do with their arms and hands. They know they have to do something but they are unsure what. They know they can't just leave their arms dangling like they aren't attached to their shoulders. So they either have a repertoire of clichés they trot out or they have one particular gesture they use over and over. Holding an invisible beach ball, clasping or praying hands, arms up and down symmetrically. It's a stereotype of an opera singer acting seen most nights in most opera houses.

One well-known singer lifts one arm in a pseudo-balletic position at the end of every aria. There is no meaning in such a gesture.

Quite often singers don't know enough about how to move in Period costume. I once witnessed a truly excellent singing soprano wearing an Empire line dress moving about like a tomboy. If she'd only known the reason why the Empire line (different countries had different names for this era, Empire, Regency, Biedermeier, Federal etc.) developed she might have started thinking differently about how she moved in that lovely dress. It was the one thing that was missing from what was otherwise a very good performance.

There is a growing desire among opera audiences for better acting skills and the students in conservatoires tend to want more quality acting tuition. The emphasis is still clearly very much on teaching singing in the conservatoires and I think this is absolutely right but not to the extent that a singer leaves their training without a foundation in the basics of acting and what will be required of them from the first day of rehearsal to the final performance.

Interestingly, instead of the focus on better acting, there has been a kind of vogue of late that the singer should look like the character and large and overweight singers have come under the spotlight for their size. I don't hold with this line of thinking and feel it is unfair. A singer's physical size is their business in the main, but their skills to convince us that whatever their size they are the character, they are involved in the scene and the relationships onstage is another matter altogether. It's an occasion where I feel size doesn't matter. But their skills, now they do matter very much.

There is alarm in some circles that opera audiences are declining, whether true or not, and that opera is elitist and irrelevant to modern life. I think opera is hugely relevant to our lives in the same way that Shakespeare is. But it is up to us practitioners, the conductors, directors, singers, designers, teachers, everyone involved in production to make it so.

So now, what exactly are the Acting Skills opera singers need to know?

Introduction

What is an Artist?

Have you ever asked yourself this question? I'm sure there are as many answers and definitions to this question as there are artists but specifically for singers in opera I think it can be answered quite succinctly. As a given we know an artist creates something. But what else makes an artist?

I want you to imagine a great singer. She had the power of Birgit Nilsson, the rich creamy tones of Leontyne Price, the gorgeous agility of Joan Sutherland. She sang in a soundproof room, she was never recorded and no one ever heard her. Is she an artist? I would say she was not. She was just someone no one ever heard of.

An artist, certainly in the context of opera, is a Professional Communicator.

Sharing, expressing, giving out, communicating are all fundamental to their vocation as singers. Yes they have special skills, they have artistry, they have craft. But the sharing these unique talents, the giving out and expressing is what makes them artists.

And I would put it to you that the better the communicator, the finer the artist.

Who is the singer communicating with?

The singer is communicating with their audience. The audience is the crucial factor in an operatic performance. Without the audience there would be no opera. They must never be taken for granted, never dismissed nor overlooked. Sadly sometimes I see productions where the director is far more interested in himself and his concept than he is satisfying his audience. The audience is the most important factor in opera and they should be always be respected.

Think about it. If the audience hadn't appreciated Mozart, Wagner, Verdi, Rossini (and many, many more of course) it's very unlikely you'd have ever heard of them.

Who is in the audience?

I want you to imagine 3 people are sitting the back row of the Gods, this is the nickname given to the highest tier of the opera house (or theatre) by theatre folk.

Those tiny dots up there in the Gods are fee-paying customers.

Our Three Friends in the Gods

1) One is blind.

2) One is deaf.

3) One cannot understand the language the opera is sung in and there are no surtitles. (Surtitles are the translation of the libretto usually projected above the stage during the performance).

Let's imagine what an opera performance will be like for each of those three audience members.

The blind audience member can only hear the singing. They can hear all the textures and colours in the voice. They can hear the depth of emotion and the heart of the singer as well as how intelligently the singer is interpreting the role. Anything that can be appreciated aurally. So for the sake of argument it might be like listening to a live recording of an opera with your eyes closed.

The deaf audience member can only see the action. They can see the story unfold, they can witness the characters and the relationships between the characters develop. They can only take in the visual. To drive this home, you might look at clips of opera performances with the sound off. This is what their experience would be like.

Our final audience member can hear and see the performance but cannot understand via the words in the libretto what is going on. All they can rely on are what they hear and are being shown on the stage. The voice and the visuals but not necessarily with any meaning. Again you might watch clips of an opera without surtitles to get an idea of what it would be like for this person. At the age of 12 when I first saw La Traviata at the San Diego Opera in 1971 this was how I experienced it. I concentrated very hard to work out what was going on.

The job of the Professional Communicator Opera Singer

Your job is to reach each of these three audience members equally. They have paid for their tickets just like everyone else. They deserve to have a rich and entertaining experience in the opera house as much as anyone else. With your skill, artistry, passion, imagination, craftsmanship and much more, your job is to deliver to all three a thrilling and engrossing performance by expressing and showing the story, the character and their relationships aurally and visually. And do it with the highest standards of craftsmanship, quality and taste.

Aha! How do you do that?

Our ancestors passing the time.

Let's start at the very beginning of the history of the Western theatrical tradition. I want you to imagine our ancestors sitting around the fire at the mouth of a cave. Historians tell us this is the place where Theatre as we know it in the West began. They tell us that it was here that ritual began. And what else did they do to while away the long hours? Historians tell us they told each other stories. Storytelling is at the very origin of the Western theatrical tradition. And it is in the DNA of Opera.

So let's jump ahead now a few hundred thousand years to 5th Century Greece. A member of the Chorus stepped out of the group and spoke as an individual for the first time. His name was Thespis and it is from him we get the term for an actor, 'thespian'. Prior to Thespis's innovation, the Chorus spoke in unison. Chanting or speaking, it was entirely in unison. But now we have something truly remarkable. We have a dialogue between the Chorus and an individual. And what do we have when we have a dialogue? We have many more creative opportunities to tell a story.

Part I - The Story

The Story in an Opera

Think of the best opera performances you have ever seen. What was it about them you enjoyed so much? I'm sure the singing was very good for you to remember it. But what else? Could it have been because they told you the story of the opera particularly well? Did they surprise you? Did they enchant you? Did they draw you into the drama, the passion, the excitement of what was happening on the stage? Did you rather like a child at storybook time feel deeply involved in what was going on? I've been going to the Opera for 47 years and the opera performances I remember loving are the ones that told me the story really well, like it was the first time it had ever been told and were able to surprised me, even if I had seen that opera many times before.

And the performances that I can look back on as not great were the ones which didn't bother to tell me the story afresh. They had decided we already knew this opera and this story. They decided it didn't matter if I understood what was going on, or they trotted out a lot of clichés, they skipped important plot points, they made assumptions about what we in the audience knew and didn't know. They just didn't bother and what they created is what I call 'dead opera'. What a pity.

There is something quite magical about storytelling. If you get it right, your audience will become a bit like children, eager to hear, see and witness what happens next, constantly surprised by the twists and turns of the plot. We all know the story of Romeo and Juliet. If it's told well, where the characters clearly do not know what is going to happen to them and if they fight every step of the way for a happy ending, the outcome is absolutely heartbreaking. But if the actors signal to the audience either unconsciously or through lack of skill that they know the outcome, then we can all go home early and skip the last scenes. They already told us how it's going to end.

Find that child inside you that loves to play

PLAY

What do you as an acting opera singer need to be able to tell a story well? You have to be able to **PLAY**. When you were a child did you play pirates, princesses, kings, wizards, animals, monsters, knights, queens, dragons, soldiers etc? That ability to play is crucial to storytelling and vital to acting in opera.

And make sure that you (like that child) takes play very seriously.

Let's look now at the structure of a story. Most stories have these three components.

- The Beginning
- The Middle
- The End

Breaking it down a bit more what needs to happen in the Beginning? This is the Introduction. So our audience needs to learn things like, who are the characters? What are their relationships to each other? Where are we, i.e. location, setting etc? What period in time are we in? What time of year, time of day?

The second part of a story, the Middle part is the Conflict. So who wants what from whom? Who wants something from another character they cannot or refuse to give. It could be information, it could be money, it could be power or control, it would be anything. But the conflict comes when one character wants something from another and cannot get it.

And lastly we have the End. The Resolution. What happens? Who wins, who loses? What is the outcome of the struggle?

For the sake of simplicity let's take the fairy tale Little Red Riding Hood to start. Read this story aloud looking out for the three components.

Little Red Riding-Hood

Once upon a time, there was a little darling damsel, whom everybody loved and her old granny loved her best of all. Once Granny made her a hood and cape of red wool for her, and since it became her so well and she would wear nothing else, people gave her the name of "Little Red Riding- Hood."

One day her mother said to her, "Here is a slice of cake and a bottle of wine; carry them to old Granny. She is ill and weak, and they will refresh her. But don't stray from the path, otherwise you will fall and break the bottle, and then poor Granny will have nothing."

Now Granny lived out in a forest, an hour's walk from the village. When Little Red Riding-Hood went into the forest, she met a wolf. But she did not know what a wicked beast he was, and was not afraid of him.

"God help you, Little Red Riding-Hood!" said he.
"God bless you, wolf!" replied she.
"Whither so early?"
"To Granny."
"What have you there under your mantle?"
"Cake and wine. We baked yesterday; old Granny must have a good meal to build up her strength."
"Where does your granny live?"
"A good quarter of an hour's walk further in the forest, under yon three large oaks. There stands her house.

The wolf thought to himself, "This nice young damsel is a rich morsel. She will taste better than the old woman; but you must trick her cleverly, that you may catch both."
For a time he walked by her side. Then said he, "Little Red Riding-Hood! Just look! There are such pretty flowers here! Why don't you look round at them all? And can you hear how delightfully the birds are singing!

Little Red Riding-Hood lifted up her eyes, and when she saw how the sun's rays glistened through the tops of the trees, and every place was full of flowers, she thought herself, "If I bring with me a sweet smelling nosegay to Granny, it will cheer her. It is still so early, that I shall come to her in plenty of time," and so she skipped into the forest and looked for flowers. And when she had plucked one, she fancied that another further off and went deeper and deeper into the forest.

But the wolf went by the straight road to old granny's, and knocked at the door.

"Who's there?"

"Little Red Riding-Hood, who has brought cake and wine. Open!"

"Only press the latch," cried Granny. "I am so weak that I cannot stand."

The wolf pressed the latch, walked in, and went without saying a word straight to granny's bed and ate her up. Then he took her clothes from her wardrobe, dressed himself in them, put her cap on his head, drew the curtains and got in her bed..

Meanwhile Little Red Riding-Hood was running after flowers, and when she had so many that she could not carry any more, she remembered granny, and started on the way to her.

It seemed strange to her that the door was wide open, and when she entered the room everything seemed to her so peculiar. "She said, "Good-day!" but received no answer.

Thereupon she went to the bed and opened the curtains. There lay granny, with her cap drawn down over her eyes, and looking so strange!

"Ah, granny! Why have you such long ears?"

"The better to hear you."

"Ah, granny! Why have you such large eyes?"

"The better to see you."

"But, granny! Why have you such a terribly large mouth?"

"The better to eat you!"

Then the wolf sprang out of bed and ate poor Little Red Riding-Hood right up. When the wolf had satisfied his appetite, he lay down again in the bed, and began to snore very loudly.

A huntsman came past, and thought to himself, "How can an old woman snore like that? I'll just have a look to see what it is."

He went into the room, and looked into the bed; there lay the wolf. "I found you now, you old rascal!" said he. "I've long been looking for you!"

He was just going to take aim with his gun, when he thought to himself, "Perhaps the wolf has swallowed granny, and she may yet be released."

So he took an axe and chopped the wolf clean in half. He saw a red hood gleam, and out skipped Little Red Riding-Hood, who cried, "Oh, how frightened I have been; it was so dark inside that wolf!"

Afterwards out came old granny, still alive, but scarcely able to breathe.

Now, they were all three merry. The huntsman took the wolf's skin; granny ate the cake and drank the wine which her granddaughter had brought, and became strong and well again; and little Red Red Riding-Hood thought to herself, "As long as I live, I won't stray from the path into the forest, when mother has forbidden me."

***

So where do you think these three components fit into this story? Where does the Introduction end and the Conflict begin? Where does the Resolution of the Conflict happen?

These things can be subjective but for my money, in this story the Conflict begins with the arrival of the Wolf. He is the character causing the trouble. He is the problem and he provides the conflict. And the Resolution? I think the Resolution starts with the arrival of the Huntsman.

Let's dissect one of Aesop's Fables.

<u>Androcles and the Lion</u>

This story takes place in Rome, where a Greek slave named Androcles escaped from his master and fled into the forest. There he wandered for a long time until he was weary and worn out with hunger and despair. Just then he heard a lion near him moaning and groaning and at times roaring terribly. Tired as he was, Androcles rose up and rushed away; but as he made his way through the bushes he stumbled over the root of a tree and fell down. When he tried to get up, he saw the lion coming towards him.

Poor Androcles was in despair; he was too weak to run away. But instead of attacking him, the lion just moaned and groaned. Androcles saw that the lion was holding out his right paw, which was covered with blood and very swollen. Looking more closely, Androcles could see a great big thorn pressed into the paw, which was the cause of all the lion's trouble. Plucking up courage he seized hold of the thorn and pulled it out of the lion's paw, who roared with pain, but soon after found such relief that he fawned on Androcles and showed his gratitude in every way that he knew.

But one day a number of soldiers came marching through the forest and found Androcles. As he could not explain what he was doing alone in the woods, they took him prisoner and brought him back to the city. Here his master soon found him and brought him before the authorities. Androcles was condemned to death for running away. It was the Roman custom to throw murderers, renegade slaves and other criminals to the lions in a huge circus for public entertainment.

So Androcles was led into the Arena with only a flimsy spear to protect himself. The Emperor was in the royal box that day and gave the signal for the lion to come out and attack Androcles. But when it was released from its cage and rampaged towards him, what do you think happened? Instead of attacking Androcles, it stopped and fawned upon him and stroked him with its paw and made no attempt to do him any harm.

It was the lion which Androcles had met in the forest. The Emperor, surprised at seeing such strange behavior in so cruel a beast, summoned Androcles to him and asked him how it happened that this particular lion had lost all its cruelty of disposition. Androcles told the Emperor all that had happened to him and how the lion was showing its gratitude for his having relieved it of the thorn. Thereupon the Emperor pardoned Androcles and ordered his master to set him free, while the lion was taken back into the forest and let loose to enjoy his liberty once more.

***

This one is a little more challenging. Where does the Introduction end and the Conflict begin? Is it when the Lion appears? Or is it before that when Androcles runs away?

I think that these plot points are still part of the Introduction. I think the Conflict begins with the arrival of the Roman soldiers that capture Androcles and take him back to Rome.

And the Resolution? In this story I think there are two parts here. First is when the Lion recognises Androcles and secondly when the Emperor frees Androcles.

These sections all have a relationship to each other. Think of it this way. Look at the Resolution and look carefully at the information in it you need to know beforehand for it to make sense. Any information that you need to know to make sense of the ending has to be somewhere in the Introduction.

So in terms of an opera performance, all those introductory details have to be clearly and subtly shown to the audience. Sometimes opera performances gloss over these points, they feel the audience must already know this, why bother showing them? Careless and poor storytelling and will lead you eventually to a dead performance.

Most operas (but not all) start slowly to give the singer and the director a chance to show the audience the setting, period, characters etc. Make use of that time to show these elements.

Again I want to make the point that you want to get your audience into a kind of childlike frame of mind. You want to engrosse and enchant them by drawing them into the action. If you make assumptions, if you skip introductory details, if you fail to explain who is who and what their relationships are to each other so the audience can't work out what is going on, they will sit back and it's just that much harder to draw them in again and if you do it too many times then they will give up and instead of feeling like participants in the performance, they will feel like passive observers and again you have a dead opera on your hands.

There is a direct relationship between you being able to play like a child and the audience falling under your engrossing spell and entering that childlike frame of mind themselves while watching you.

Storytelling in More detail:

Beginning:

1) You need to show and explain to the audience: the setting, who is who (very important), where you are, what your relationship is to the other characters (also very important). Time of day, time of year, period, the society you are in. Show your audience these things. Never assume because this is a well-known opera that your audience already knows the story and you only need to go through the motions half-heartedly. Many of these elements can be done with the set, the costumes and the lighting but ask yourself, 'Is there something I can add?' Shaking out an umbrella which would show the audience it is raining outside, taking your gloves off could show it is cold outside, or putting on a sun hat to show the audience it is very sunny outside, to how you move in your costume, to a gentle pat on the cheek showing a

relationship of motherly love to your child. The possibilities are endless. Don't make a meal out of this by the way. Subtlety is everything here.

Tell the whole story

Don't cheat the audience and don't cheat your performance. Operas tend to be slow at the beginning which is deliberate in order to give you the opportunity to show these details. Take your time and show them. When your character appears for the first time, be sure you 'introduce' yourself to the audience.

The Conflict - The Problem

2) What does your character want? Who or what is preventing your character from getting
what they want? Or who wants something from you that you don't want to give? What strategies and tactics can your character use to get what they want? How can you put off that person and avoid giving in? What can your character do to win? In an opera like Rigoletto or Tosca, there has to be plenty at stake and playing this fully is crucial to a successful performance.

The End

3) The Resolution of the Conflict. Did I get what I wanted? How did I get it? If I lost, why? Who are the winners and the losers? Remember: Your character does not know how the opera ends and you must play it for the best outcome the character would want to the very end. Never play a scene like you know how it will end. Create surprise. And the audience needs to see clearly what happens in the outcome of the opera*.

*I once saw a production of Tosca at a world famous opera company in which as Tosca mounted the steps to leap off the battlements of the Castel Sant'Angelo, a huge portcullis descended and then a group of soldiers all crowded up against it and that was all we saw. We did not see Tosca leap. Gosh what a let down.

At another production in an outdoor performance in Italy I attended, Tosca mounted the steps, sang her final line about meeting Scarpia before God and flung herself off in full view of the audience and disappeared, her dress fluttering in the wind behind her. It was magnificent, incredibly dramatic and the audience went bonkers. Please directors and singers, show the outcome clearly to the audience.

My teacher at drama school made a very interesting point about the end of Romeo and Juliet which the year above us had put on. He reminded us that at the very end of the play, when the parents, the Prince, the entire town are staring in utter disbelief at the bodies of these two young people in the Capulet crypt, Friar Lawrence steps forward and says:

"Romeo, there dead, was husband to that Juliet,
And she, there dead, that Romeo's faithful wife.
I married them".

Alas, as my teacher pointed out, the actors on the stage stood there unmoved and silent. This is News to everyone and it's really terrible news adding so much pain to the loss of these beautiful young people. The people of Verona had no idea that the children of the two enemy families could possibly be married. It's so shocking and so sad. No one could stand there unmoved in that situation. Show the full impact of the ending.

Storytelling in Opera is all about Teamwork

Team Storytelling Exercise:

Divide up a fairy tale (or any good story) into three of four readers and tell the story highlighting the three elements of Beginning, Middle and End. Storytelling is all about teamwork. You cannot tell the story as well on your own no matter how hard you try. I once witnessed rehearsals where a singer had worked out their entire performance before they had even met the other cast members. They would even provide reactions and responses before the cues because it had all been worked out in their mind long before rehearsals began. S/he did manage eventually to get the timing right but because they were in a kind of bubble, they were in her own world and as the run continued, their performance lost its way. Stick to the team. Work as a team when you tell the story. Don't plan every reaction out ahead of time. You don't know what the other singers are going to give you to work with to build your performance until you are rehearsing with them.

Important Points:

- Play the story like it is the first time it has ever been told.
- Make no assumptions.
- Explain/show the details in the introduction.
- What does your character know and not know?
- Don't predict the outcome of the story.

Visual Storytelling Exercise

Now let's take on Team storytelling from another angle. Remember we are telling the story visually. So why not choose another story, a fairytale or whatever you choose. I have used fairy tales, Greek myths, even the dumbshow from Hamlet for this. Cast your story, every character must be represented. Let your imagination soar. Cast the trees, cast the wind, cast the mountains, the bridge, anything and everything that helps tell the story. Choose a narrator and have your actors show us the story visually while the narrator reads it aloud. The narrator must be very careful to follow the actors to allow them time to show us what is going on. Give us full and realistic characters. They do not speak but remember this is not Marcel Marceau mime, these are real characters. What can you show our Three Friends in the Gods? Particularly the deaf one?

Now combine the two exercises into one with several readers in one group standing behind the audience and cast all the roles as above in another group telling the story visually, and let's see both groups working closely together as one team. Again make sure your readers don't rush the actors. Give the actors plenty of time to show what is happening as the reading of the story progresses. Now switch sides so everyone gets a chance.

Give yourself somewhere to go

Your character within the opera has a story progression, a narrative, so start at the beginning and move through the progression of the story. Your character learns and develops as the story unfolds, find those moments and show those discoveries, realisations, new ideas. And this applies to each aria, scene, each act, to the entire opera.

Let's look at a character like Massenet's _Manon_. She has such a wonderful arc to play. She starts as a completely innocent schoolgirl in the 1st Act. She has no idea about men, she is pure innocence. In the 2nd Act she becomes a little more knowing, and we get a hint of her fatal flaw of avarice. It is dawning on her that she has power over men through her beauty and charms. The 3rd Act she is in her glory as the most popular courtesan in Paris and she enjoys all the attention and the fact that she really has the power to manipulate the male sex and can get whatever she wants from them. The 4th Act her craving for money has become an obsession. She can control men so now she wants more and more money. In the 5th and final Act she has destroyed herself with her greed and selfishness. The changes and character development should be clear and subtle in each act and between acts so you take the audience with you. If you make too big a change from scene to scene or from one act to the other you may lose your audience.

A very important point to make about a character like Manon is that she is not deliberately being selfish and destructive. This would make her very unsympathetic. She needs to be played like she cannot stop herself. She started life as an innocent young girl heading to a convent and she tries very hard to control these selfish urges but she fails. This makes her a sympathetic soul. The more she tries and the more she fails the more we as the audience will care about her.

Basic exercise for Introduction and Scene-setting skills.

By imagining your environment, show us:

- Where you are.

- What time of day.

- The weather.

- Who is who?

Suggested scenarios:

Finding a nice spot to sit on your blanket and read a book at the beach.
The waiting room at the Doctor's surgery.
Coming home from work and relaxing in front of the television.
Looking at paintings at an art gallery.
Sitting at a table at a restaurant and trying to get the waiter's attention.

Imagine the scene. Use your senses. There's no need to speak but this is not mime. It requires you to use your imagination and see as much as you can in minute detail. From the texture and feel of the sand, to the colour of the beach blanket, to the wall paper in the waiting room to the different paintings you can see and where they are placed on the wall to what kind of food you are going to order. Choose as much as you can before you start and let the rest come to you. Free and involve the whole galaxy of your imagination!

And remember to show us what you think and how you feel about this setting.

The Conflict

CONFLICT Means CONTACT

USE ACTIONS TO GET WHAT YOU WANT

And make contact with the other characters by using Actions.

Actions are always simple active verbs that can be expressed directly to another character. I want to - charm, threaten, comfort, tease, cajole, patronise, seduce, insult, dismiss, plead, flirt, beg, attack and so forth. There are thousands of action verbs to use, each very specific. Remember this is an active verb you can do to another character. Verbs which will not help you are those such as 'to like', 'to think', 'to look', 'to smile', 'to long for'. It has to be a verb which you can do to another character. They instantly create Contact like an electrical connection.

This is how we get what we want in real life. When a child wants an ice cream, they focus directly on the parent as they beg, they plead, they demand, they insist, they threaten, they challenge. When we want something badly enough we will try every tactic. When you use an action on another character you want to get a reaction or response from them. When they react then you know you have reached them and you are getting somewhere. This striving for Contact is something a singer should do every time they sing.

Ask yourself what effect are the actions having on the other characters? Are you making FULL CONTACT? (i.e. head, heart and guts)

Action Exercise

Choose an action (in my lessons I have each example action on a flashcard), show us that action to another person saying simply numbers or letters or if you are really advanced without any sound and without miming! Make contact!

The point of this exercise is to separate out the action from the words so as much as possible we just see the action. Operative word here is 'see'. Those watching might even cover their ears so they just see the action. Is it reading to the audience? Can you work out what the Action is? Up to the group to decide if the action is clear and full.

Later once you have grasped this concept you can apply it to phrases of music. In Act II, Tosca pleads, she demands, she protests, she begs, she confronts, she deflects, she avoids, she repels, she tests, she charms, she does many, many actions to convince Baron Scarpia to free her lover.

Exercise for the Conflict
Show us what you want and your tactics and play to win!

● A friend wants to borrow money.
● Two co-workers argue about who has done the most work on a project.
● A young girl has disobeyed her father.
● Sisters struggle over care of their elderly Parent.

Try adding actions to this exercise. Begging, demanding, insulting, confronting, rejecting, rebelling, attacking, contradicting, charming, praising, soothing, patronising and of course many more. Remember like anything in the Story, conflict has progression. Conflicts tend to start small and grow. Conflicts can also ebb and flow.

Make sure these Actions elicit a physical response going back and forth between the players.

This exercise can be very good for students who are not used to experiencing conflict to have the opportunity to explore what it is like to really disagree with another character. This can be challenging in some cultures. Being able to play a conflict is a skill like any other. Once you've finished this exercise, I suggest the students make up and just remind themselves it is only an exercise.

As in an opera performance, you can get very involved in the action but as a professional once you step off the magic space of the stage you leave the drama there, and you can relax and have a cup of tea in your dressing room! Remember this is **Play**. It is Make-Believe!

You may not feel you need to assign an action to every line or phrase. That's absolutely fine. But you might feel stuck in a scene and you could ask yourself. 'What do I want and what am I doing to her/him/them to get it in this phrase or section?' Finding the right action will clarify that for you.

(N.b. I want to thank the brilliant Lenore DeKoven who I studied with at UCLA for the concept of Actions).

The End:

Show the outcome. Show us the winners and the losers. Surprise us, show us that this result was not inevitable. Show us the spontaneous decisions being made that lead to this unexpected outcome.

Visual Storytelling

Find YouTube clips of operatic performances in which the visual storytelling is especially good. Look at the the the superb Diana Damrau singing Der Holle Rache from the excellent Royal Opera House production of The Magic Flute directed by Sir David McVicar. There is so much terrific visual work in this scene. The Contact between the Queen of the Night and her daughter Pamina is so clear and tangible. You see the Queen rejecting, dominating, threatening, controlling, daring, challenging. Turn the sound off when you watch it. Ms. Damrau is so riveting to watch and is just superb as is Sir David's entire production. This is fully alive opera!

12

Part II

Character and Relationships

This is the Who of your performance. Who are you? What kind of person are you? What is your background? What is your identity as a person? This is so much fun to explore. I suggest you do this homework long before you start rehearsals. Delve into the life of your character and find the person you are portraying. Play is very important here. Imagine and Play this person. Here your playful child who loved to play Kings, soldiers, Empresses, monsters, animals, cars, talking trees, wizards, magical elves, and so much more becomes involved. Really draw that playful you into the picture now. Most people today to earn a crust must sit in front of a computer all day. You are one of the most lucky people in the world. You make your living by playing. This is your time for Make Believe, for 'What if?' to set you imagination free.

Establishing Your Character

Do your homework:

● Study the music and the libretto from the dramatic point of view and better to do it while you are learning the music

● Learn about the period the opera was written and the period it is set if different

Learn as much as you can about the opera. And study the life of the composer.

Case in point: Verdi and La Traviata

I'm often amazed how few singers know why Verdi wrote _La Traviata_.

Have a look at this timeline.

1840 - Verdi's wife and two children are dead. Verdi is devastated

1842 - Verdi meets Giuseppina Strepponi a soprano, unmarried mother of at least 3 children by two different men, during the La Scala production of Nabucco.

1846 - Strepponi moves to Paris to teach singing

1847 - Verdi has joined Giuseppina in Paris and they move in together

1852 - The couple see a theatrical version of the Dumas novel La Dame aux Camellias. Verdi immediately starts writing La Traviata.

1853 - In just 12 months La Traviata is first performed.

1859 - Giuseppina and Giuseppi become Mr and Mrs Verdi

1897 - Giuseppini dies

1901 - Verdi dies

So as Verdi sat in the theatre watching _La Dame aux Camelias_, who do you think he was imagining as his Marguerite? It seems pretty obvious to me that he was seeing his beloved Giuseppina on that stage. A woman who was rejected by society because she hadn't followed the rules. I believe La Traviata is a plea for compassion and acceptance for a 'fallen woman' who was the love of his life.

Historically composers had many reasons for writing an opera. Some were purely commercial and some were labours of love. Worth doing your research about this.

Read and study the background texts, i.e. _Don Giovanni_, _Barber of Seville_, _Tosca_, _Madame Butterfly_, _Boris Godunov_, _Billy Budd_, _Marriage of Figaro_, _La Traviata_ and many, many more are based on original plays or stories.

A singer once made an interesting point about background texts of operas. He said they can be confusing because they are often so different or have a different structure to the opera story. He was right in that they can be different but it's worth looking at them to find out why. The novella the Bizet opera _Carmen_ is based on by Prosper Merimée is quite different from Henri Meilhac's libretto. In the original story Don Jose is a ruthless if charming highwayman, he kills Carmen's husband, he's on the run and is finally condemned when found guilty of murdering Carmen. But we also get some extremely useful information about him in the original story. He was studying to be a priest in the Basque region of Spain when he killed a man in a dispute over a game of chance. He then joined the army and was posted as far away as possible to Seville in Andalucia. When you are creating your character of Don Jose, you might just want look at those differences. I think Bizet wanted Don Jose to be a much more sympathetic character than he is in the original story. In the opera, he starts out a very decent, strictly by the book army officer. And little by little as each scene progresses he loses his moral bearings and eventually becomes a deranged man who murders a woman in broad daylight in the final scene. We want to portray Don Jose in the first scene like this would be an absolutely inconceivable outcome for him in the final scene of the last act. He fights to maintain control of himself every step of the way from his first entrance to his final disastrous act. Look at the original story. More can become clear than you can find in the libretto. For those sopranos lucky enough to sing the role of Puccini's Tosca, I would say it is imperative that she reads Sardou's original play written for the great actress Sarah Bernhardt. In the play you understand why

Floria Tosca is tempestuous, religious and a singer. In the play we are told that Tosca was discovered by monks on the side of a mountain tending sheep as a small child. They take her in and teach her music. So there we have it. She was a feral child, she was taught religion and music by monks. And she's still a bit of a wild child.

Character study based on your research sources.

Look for clues to their:

● Social Status & Money

● Family & Childhood

● Intellect & Beliefs

● Physicality of the character*

*I once saw a young singer delivering Sister Prejean's aria from the opera based on the film Dead Man Walking. She was a very fit young woman and had a powerfully athletic physical presence. I felt she was too athletic and physical for the portrayal of a nun. Nuns tend to focus on the spiritual side of living and do not in general have the physicality of an acrobat. Perfect for a trouser role but not a nun. It could be an easy adjustment to make and would make a big difference to the believability of your performance. If you are playing a nun, and there are several operas with nuns in them, I would do my research and sit in on some convent vesper services. You could glean a lot of useful information about your character's way of life.

In each scene...

When you enter, know where you have come from, where you are going and know where you are going on your exit. Is there something with a prop or a piece of business you can use to 'show' any of these things?

If you enter and take off your hat and shake it out a bit then your audience will know that it's wet outside. If you are a lovely lady in a beautiful dress and you are closing a parasol as you enter then the audience will learn you that you are a delicate woman who does not wish to get too much sun.

The possibilities for this are endless but make sure they are directly related to the character and the storytelling, are subtle and are showing the audience rather than clobbering them over the head by 'telling' them.

Play and show the Relationships

Relationships between the characters are so very important in the telling of the story. Let's look at Cio-Cio San and Suzuki in Madama Butterfly. Cio-Cio San is younger than Suzuki. But as the mistress of the house and the mother of the child she has higher status. But they are also close friends. And Suzuki knows in her heart that Cio-Cio San is deluded in her dedication to Pinkerton. It's a complex and very interesting relationship and for the opera to work, these things have to be clear to the audience. Similarly we can imagine that Sharpless is older than Pinkerton, but he is somehow rather passive in comparison to the adventurous naval officer. Sharpless warns his friend about his attitude to this nice young Japanese girl. Pinkerton and Cio-Cio San are quite headstrong characters who do not or cannot listen.

Play the situation and the relationships

● Where am I?

● Who's also here and what are my relationships to them?

● Who has higher and lower status and why?

● Who are my friends and who are my enemies? Do I know the difference?

● How do the relationships change? Has trust developed? Growing curiosity? Fear? Love?

● How are changes in the situation and the relationships moving the story on?

● Am I 'showing'* these things?

*Let me give you an example of 'showing' rather than 'telling' the audience. I once sat in on rehearsals for an opera in which a character, a very posh gentleman poet had just climbed a steep hill. Upon entering, the excellent tenor playing this role didn't do something obvious like fan himself with his hat. He took out a perfectly pressed pocket square from his jacket pocket and touched his forehead in two places and then gently dabbed the back of his neck. This is how a gentleman copes with perspiration. Such a clever touch. Think it through. What can you show the audience about the character and the scene in a simple and subtle way?

Use your imagination

● Fill in the gaps with your imagination. If there is nothing else to go on, create a backstory for the character that fits the plot.

Know and show the character development.

Your character goes on a journey. They start at one place and end up at another destination, either physically, emotionally, intellectually or all three. They change. It's crucial to show the changes in the story.

● What was I like before the curtain went up?

● How do I change in each act?

● How am I different from the 1st scene to the final curtain?

● Have learnt anything?

● Have I matured or grown up?

● Have I aged?

Individuate your character.

An important part of playing the relationships in an opera is working out similarities and differences between the characters.

● How am I similar to the other characters and how am I different?

● What qualities do we have in common and what makes me different?

Examples: Character groupings. In many productions I have seen, these characters are often far too similar. There's so much to be had from creating differences between them to enhance the story.

● The Three Ladies in *The Magic Flute*. Why are they always the same?

● Mercedes and Frasquita in *Carmen* are often cardboard cutouts of each other.

● Ping, Pang and Pong in *Turandot*. Never seen it once where they were different and each of these characters has a very different job in the palace.

● The Rhinemaidens in _Rhinegold_. Wonderful opportunities here for the characters to be different from each other.

● The three courtesans in _La Rondine_. I sat in on rehearsals for a production of this opera once and it was fascinating to watch the three excellent singers in these roles individuate their characters. There is absolutely nothing in the score or libretto giving any clue to any differences between them. So the singers used their own personalities. One was lofty, superior and rather grand, one was very sensitive and soulful and one was very energetic and a bit pugnacious. And what did they have as courtesans in common? Men and money. Anytime a man appeared their radar went up. And they found a brilliant moment without distracting from the action when they compared jewellery that men had given them. Earrings, rings and bracelets. Such a great touch and showed the audience so much!

Couples: Some similarities and differences.

● Tosca and Cavaradossi

What do these two characters have in common? First of all they are both artists. This could be part of what draws them together. But Cavaradossi is leading a secret life as a political activist. But he never tells Tosca about his political activities. And in Act I Tosca is troubled that she heard her lover talking to someone as she entered the church earlier which he denies. She returns later to check up on him where she bumps into Baron Scarpia. So we can glean that as much as they love each other, they don't really trust each other. In the play you discover that Caravadossi is a republican and Tosca supports the Queen of Naples which is why he doesn't tell her what he is up to. And Tosca's first experience of the world was very insecure so trust is a big issue for her.

● Carmen and Don Jose

Carmen is a gypsy. She is an outsider. She lives only for today. She does and says exactly what she wants. Don Jose is an army officer. He has strict regulations to obey. He is a good respectable Catholic Spaniard who follows all the rules. And how are they similar? As mentioned previously Don Jose has committed a murder in the original story. He has form for losing control. Under the veneer of respectability is a very passionate and potentially dangerous man.

● Butterfly and Pinkerton

Butterfly and Pinkerton both exist in very controlled environments. Butterfly as the daughter of a disgraced father, and a woman in 19th century Japan lives in a very proscribed little world. Pinkerton as a lieutenant on a US Naval vessel is subject to navy regulations and a very structured life aboard ship. So what are they hoping for from each other? Some kind of freedom. A way to get out from under all the control which is oppressing them. What else do they have in common? They are both very stubborn people who will not be told. They both think they understand each other's cultures and they do not. It is the very basis of the tragedy.

● Fiordiligi and Dorabella in _Cosi fan tutte_

Often these characters are played as too much alike. Two sisters. Both spoilt and rather selfish. Interesting to note there is no parent figure in their household. Looking carefully at the libretto there are clues to differences between these two ladies. In response to the romantic approaches of the two 'Albanians' Fiordiligi says her loyalty to her lover is 'Like a Rock'. She is a bit self-righteous. She mentions her Christian faith. You start to see something of the responsible older sister in this aria. Dorabella on the other hand is very quick to set aside her feelings for Ferrando and gives in to the advances of her suitor. She has less self-control and is very easily convinced. Singers playing these roles might explore an almost mother/daughter relationship between these two sisters. There is no parent figure in their house. Could Fiordiligi be fulfilling that role to some extent? This would add a very interesting dynamic to the story and make it much richer for the audience.

● Donna Anna and Donna Elvira in *Don Giovanni*

I have seen many productions where these two characters could be cardboard cutouts of each other and it's very hard to tell one from the other. Donna Anna and Donna Elvira are both ladies of high social standing. Donna Anna in this context translated to Lady Anna as an English title of nobility. There is something very obsessive and obsessional about both of these ladies. They cannot let go and pursue Don Giovanni with a vengeance. But there are differences in their motivation. The assaulted and bereaved Donna Anna is out for revenge and wants to see Don Giovanni punished. She slavishly focuses on her goal and will not let go until this man gets his just deserts. Donna Elvira on the other hand, is in the modern vernacular, a 'woman who loves too much'. She has been so poorly treated by the Don and yet her real motivation (if sometimes hidden by her vanity) is to get him back. The kind of woman who is drawn to a man who mistreats her. They are not the same characters. There are similarities between them but also big differences.

You may not agree with me about these particular observations. They are subjective. But the concept is worth applying. Find the similarities and the differences between characters. Adds a huge amount of depth to the story if you do.

Know and show the character development

● What was I like before the curtain went up?

● How do I change in each act?

● How am I different from the 1st scene to the final curtain?

● Have learnt anything?

● Have I matured or grown up?

● Have I aged?

Relationship exercise

Without speaking (and not miming) show us a relationship:

- Father/Daughter

- Husband/Wife

- Teacher/Student

- Servant/Master

- Brother/Sister

- Two old friends

- A princess and a duchess

Remember to show not only the relationship but how the individuals think and feel about each other.

For the purposes of this exercise, I suggest you don't speak. This is not Marcel Marceau mime. Find a reason in the improvisation that speech is not required. For instance a scenario I use sometimes is a daughter introducing her parents to her sleeping baby for the first time. She opens the door to the nursery very quietly, she leads her parents over to the crib and they tiptoe in and very gently lean over to peer at the sleeping child. They are overjoyed but dare not make a sound! Then they quietly step out being very careful not to wake the baby. The parents are so proud of their daughter. They are delighted to be grandparents. They fall in love with this baby. So here three actors can show the relationships between four people. Husband and Wife, Mother and Daughter, Father and Daughter, Grandparents and baby.

Mother and baby. And this can easily be done in about 90 seconds.

18

A Storytelling and Relationship combined exercise:

Taking a little bit of dramatic licence for the sake of the exercise, at the beginning of Act III of Puccini's *Manon Lescaut*, Manon and a group of other women are at the French port of Le Havre being transported to Louisiana having been found guilty of immorality and prostitution.

Set the scene. It's a port. Where is the dock? Where is the gangway? Where's the ship? Where are the soldiers who are in charge of these prisoners, where are the women?

A soldier reads out the names of the women one by one. The women are on one side of the stage as as their names are called, one by one they must cross the stage in this walk of shame and step up the gangway and board the ship.

Rosetta!
Madelon!
Manon!
Ninetta!
Caton!
Regina!
Claretta!
Violetta!
Nerina!
Elisa!

Ninon!
Giorgetta!

Every one of these ladies should have a different backstory. For the sake of the exercise, let's say one is deeply ashamed, one is very defiant, one is ill and can barely walk, one flaunts herself outrageously, one is very bitter this has happened to her, one is completely deranged, one is petrified with fear, let's say two are sisters and when one is named they both try to cross together but soldiers won't allow that and they are separated which causes them huge distress. Use your imagination and give each woman a character and a different backstory. Are they different ages and from different social classes? How do they feel about each other? How do they feel about these soldiers? And what about the soldiers? How do they feel about this job? One might be very sympathetic to their plight but doesn't want to show it to his comrades, one might really enjoy ogling all these women of ill repute, one might just be doing his job. It is in the moving, the crossing of the stage that the opportunity to really show these things can happen.

We want to **see** the story, we want to **see** the characters, we want to **see** the relationships between all of the characters.

Getting the thought

Thoughts are repeatable, emotions are not. Get the thought and the emotion will follow simply and naturally.

Watch people behaving. The normal pattern that leads to speech or in the case of opera singing would be:

● Think, look, move, sing. If nothing else, THINK BEFORE YOU SING

This is a hugely important acting skill to learn and to develop. What is making you want to sing in the first place? What thought is so powerful that you want so sing it out. Use the galaxy of your imagination to create that huge powerful thought. Or find that gentle little thought for that tender note.

I don't think you can summon up anything by trying to remember an emotion. Thoughts lead to feelings. Focus on the thought and the feeling will follow. Keep your mind locked onto the thought.

Acting in Opera is **THOUGHT DRIVEN.** Find the thought of the character and allow the thought to lead.

Back to Butterfly:

From the libretto.

BUTTERFLY
He will return.

SUZUKI
Let us hope so.

BUTTERFLY

Say it with me.
He's coming back.

SUZUKI
He'll come back.

BUTTERFLY
You're crying? Whatever for?
Oh, you lack faith!
Listen.

Prior to singing her aria, Cio-Cio San
might think: "I know he is coming
back. I've never shared this with you
but I've thought of every detail of his
return and I think about it every day.
It's going to happen just like this".

These big and powerful thoughts compel her to sing out
the story of Pinkerton's return which is the famous aria:

Un bel di…

Thought exercise:

Look at the back of your hand. Look very carefully at it
and study it. Now close your eyes and see it as clearly as
you can. See your hand in minute detail. Open your
eyes again and look at your hand. Study it. Close your
eyes and see your hand in as much detail as possible.

The Lemon

Close your eyes and imagine you are standing at your
kitchen counter and before you is a big plump juicy lemon
on a chopping board. You pick up a knife and you
carefully cut that juicy lemon in half. Keeping your eyes

closed, pick up one half of the lemon and bring it up to your mouth. You can smell the sharp scent, the juice is dripping on your fingers. See the lemon. In minute detail. Now take it and give it a little squeeze and lick it. Feel all the sensations for a second or two. Now put the imaginary lemon and the knife down and open your eyes. Did your mouth water? Did you smell lemon? Did your eyes sting a bit?

Thoughts can be very powerful. They can be powerful enough give you a physical reaction. And thoughts are repeatable.

More thought work:

Close your eyes and imagine a gorgeous scene of mountains in the distance. Are there clouds, is there snow on the peaks? See it in detail. Imagine it as clearly as you can.

Now open your eyes and look out and see those mountains. See the clouds. See the peaks. See the snow There are some people who don't visualise as their primary sense which is fine. Then use your primary sense. Smell the mountain air, feel the biting cold breeze.

Now repeat seeing the mountains with your eyes closed. Commit to you memory those mountains and peaks. See them in minute detail. Then open your eyes and see the mountains again. Thoughts can be very powerful if you can train your mind to use them.

Try this exercise to create a New Idea. Show us you spontaneously have a new idea.

● You've misplaced a book and are looking for it and then find it.

● Getting home and realise you have forgotten something

● Deciding not to answer the phone

● Going through a cookbook deciding what you are going to cook tonight and then choosing the ingredients. Do you have them all?

Take it a bit further with this improvised scenario:

You have committed a crime and have left a crucial and damning piece of evidence which could be used to convict you at the scene which you have to return to find, hide, collect or destroy. You must find this evidence as quickly as possible as you don't know who might come in and catch you. So you enter very quietly, then you have the urgent search for the evidence, then you find it, then you deal with it so it will not incriminate you. Make it urgent, play it very seriously. Go through all the thought processes step by step. Decide what the evidence is before you start. A letter, a glove, a box of matches. Think about the layout of the room. Making some decisions before you start would be very helpful.

Think in pictures

Project your thoughts out over the audience. Make the entire audience space is your Imax Screen. Use the full galaxy of your imagination.   Are those thoughts clear and powerful enough to reach our three friends in the Gods?

Again Acting in Opera is **THOUGHT DRIVEN.** See your aria like a film projecting your thoughts on your Imax Screen out over the audience.

Play the Opposites

To play the situation, play the opposites.

● Where are my feelings the strongest? How do I show that?

● Where are my feelings the weakest? How do I show that?

● Find the extremes and fill in one end of them to the other.

● Find your character's most important traits and habits and fill them in. Show them.

You could use the Seven Deadly Sins

● Pride
● Envy

- Gluttony
- Lust
- Anger
- Greed
- Sloth

And combine them with the Seven Heavenly Virtues

- Faith
- Hope
- Charity
- Fortitude
- Justice
- Temperance
- Prudence

Applied practically to two characters:

Tosca:
Her sins: Pride, Envy and Anger
Her virtues: Faith, Hope and Justice

Baron Scarpia:
His sins: Pride, Lust and Greed
His virtues: Fortitude, Justice and Prudence

Do you notice anything interesting?

21
Listen for the clues the composer is giving you about the character and the action in the music.

Find the Zefferelli production of _Tosca_ on YouTube with Maria Callas and Tito Gobbi. Look at the Second Act. There are so many interesting clues that Franco Zeffirelli uses in Puccini's music. There's a big soaring phrase when Tosca sees the knife and then contemplates as a good Catholic woman if she can commit a mortal sin and kill another human being. And quiet rumbling when she puts the candles down next to the dead Scarpia and a wonderful chilling moment she uses in the music to put the crucifix down on his body. It's in the score and clearly in the music but I've rarely seen these brilliant musical clues used in a production. You could use those clues in the music but stage it entirely differently.

A very important point to make is that if the composer is giving you a musical clue to character or action, you need to fill in, provide the backup thoughts timed exactly right to make them fit with the music. You can't just do something without the thought process which leads up to it. (See above!)

So always ask yourself if the composer is telling you something important in the music.

Be sure to use everything around you to help tell the story. I saw a production of _Madama Butterfly_ where in the last act Cio-Cio San had made a little 'Pinkerton' shrine on downstage right. There was a small statue of Liberty, there was a little American flag, a Cross, some flowers. When Pinkerton finally realises what he has done and the devotion Cio-Cio San had for him he fell to his knees only a few feet from the little shrine but he never looked at it, never reacted to it. Seeing that shrine could have what brought him to his knees and perhaps he could have shared his shock and regret with Sharpless.

Sometimes something really helpful is right under your nose. Use it.

22

Note on playing heroines, heroes and villains.

Heroes: No one is all good. Show their faults but in a sympathetic way. When are they too prideful, when are they too impulsive, when are they too trusting and naive, when do they make a mistake or two?

Villains: Find the good things about the character. They think they are doing the right thing and think they are good people. Are they somehow sexy and their wickedness is attractive? Find the good in the villain. (The best Don Giovannis and Scarpias I have ever seen have been very charming and sexy. And one of the best examples of playing the opposite I've seen is Glenn Close in the film Dangerous Liaisons. As the Marquise de Merteuil, she is so genuinely caring and kind, almost saintly, while behind that mask she cruelly destroys the lives of those around her)

Play the opposites!!

To Recap:

- Put the story and the character together

- Don't cheat your performance by relying on the surtitles to do the work for you.

- Look for opportunities to show **visually** what is happening and how the drama is unfolding.

A example of some visual storytelling:

The Wedding Scene in Madama Butterfly. In this scene in late 19th century Japan, the young bride Cio-Cio San is marrying the dashing US Naval officer Benjamin Franklin Pinkerton. Everything seems to be going well until her uncle The Bonze enters. He has discovered she has secretly converted to Christianity and in his rage he curses her, tells the guests at her wedding to leave and then they all exit. Without surtitles and knowledge of the language, it would be very hard to work out what is actually happening. This scene is always more or less the same in every production I have ever seen. The cursing and then the exit of the relatives.

What if The Bonze pulled out a crucifix out of his kimono, shows her relatives this crucifix and breaks it in half and throws it down in front of Cio-Cio San. He is showing her, the relatives (and the audience) his fury that she has abandoned her traditional religion and betrayed her ancestors. This would provide a crucial visually dramatic element for such a serious moment in the opera and could add more conviction to the singing.

And actions he might use: to destroy, to humiliate, to punish, to threaten, to lecture, to hector, to attack, to insult, to shame…

If you keep our three audience members in the Gods in mind, these ideas are more likely to come to you.

Look for opportunities…

Ask yourself:

● How can I show that I am jealous?

● How can I show that I am angry?

● How can I show that I secretly love that Character?

Acting Gold Nugget:

How you treat another character's personal props shows how you feel about them. This is an acting gold mine of opportunity.

For an exercise, set out a group of props, a walking stick, a handkerchief, a toy, a glove, a letter, a scarf, a book etc.

In the exercise you discover one of these items and you remember the owner. This is the glove of your secret love. She doesn't know how much you love her. Use your senses. Touch the glove, smell the glove. All your longing for her will come out for the audience to see.

Choose the toy which could be of a kidnapped child, the scarf of a dead parent, the letter of an enemy. Show us how you feel about them by how you handle that prop.

Take your time in the exercise to explore but bear in mind in an operatic performance you may have only a few seconds to show this.

A word about comic opera

Play it seriously. Play it for truth. Play it with plenty at stake. The conflict can be approached a bit more like a game you play to win.

What is funny?

Generally playing the idiosyncratic/absurd/ridiculous combined with the unexpected will get a laugh. Signalling that a joke is coming is the best way to kill it stone dead.

Again create surprise!

This came up in a workshop once. A student asked me if my approach applied to comic opera and I was taken a bit off guard as I don't find most 'comic opera' particularly funny. For some reason the normal rules of comedy in the theatre rarely apply in performances of comic opera. Every joke is signaled in advance as if to say, 'Get ready, a joke is coming!' It's just not funny if you tell the audience in advance a joke is on its way. You have to surprise them.

A great example of real comedy in opera is a scene in Laurent Pelly's wonderful production of La Fille du Régiment. In the first act, Tonio who is in love with Marie, the 'daughter' and sort of mascot of the regiment is being interrogated by the sergeant to make sure his intentions are honourable. At one point the corpulent sergeant bumps Tonio three times with his large stomach and in the last bump Tonio goes flying and lands in a big washing basket. It's very funny because it is ridiculous and because it's totally unexpected. I wish we had more of that kind of humour in comic opera.

Part III ESSENTIAL STAGE SKILLS

These are the skills that opera singers are very rarely taught. These are basics of what used to be called 'Stage Deportment'. They are almost like a form of stage etiquette. Most classical actors know these skills and they are second nature to them. They are basic skills of how to move and how to make the most of your space on the stage. How to look professional. How to look graceful, how to adapt your body to play in a period long ago when people moved and behaved rather differently than we do now. And there are some skills which you can take into your daily life from this moment on.

The importance of Good Relaxed Upright Posture

● Pull down your bolero*

● Balance over your centre.

● Your head floats up

● Shoulders always relaxed and down

● Find your neutral position (without locking your knees)

● Ladies must avoid the 'Jeans Position'**

*A bolero is a kind of mini waistcoat or vest that matadors in Spain wear. Imagine you are wearing a bolero and someone is standing behind you and gently pulls the back of it down a bit. You might notice an improvement in your posture. Once you have worked out your good relaxed upright posture you and your voice teacher are happy with, then take it into your everyday life and make it a habit.

Good relaxed upright posture is a very important part of being a good communicator. If your chest is collapsed, or your shoulders are pushed forward, you are unlikely to sing as well as you are both mentally and physically closing down your ability to give out, to express and to share, to communicate.

** From the late 1960s onwards, we started to see women standing more like men. Wearing jeans, they started to slouch when they stood. Hip slightly out, looking a bit rebellious. This is not a good body position to take for a lady in a traditional operatic performance. Don't be a tomboy and do avoid the Jeans Position.

25

GESTURE

What is a meaningful gesture?

"A gesture is a symbolic psychological movement". Get into the psychological landscape of the character and think virtually tactile!

Watch people when they are gesturing to each other. We are not monkeys. Monkeys touch each other constantly but we've moved beyond that now. Instead we make symbolic movements which represent actual touching. Pointing for instance is often a symbolic movement representing touching another person with our index finger. Point. Him.

Or beckoning someone with your hand or your fingers. 'Come here' and the fingers move back and forth from the person with the emphasis on the towards part of the movement. In your mind you are pulling that person physically to you. But as I said we are not monkeys so we do this symbolically with our hands and arms.

Or the hand goes up as if to say 'Stop!' If we made contact it might well be a hand pushing another person's face away. But now as civilised beings we just make the symbolic movement but the other person very likely gets the point.

Meaningful gestures are always connected to the mental processes of the character. They are not the meaningless 19th century balletic movements you still so often see in the opera house.

For some reason this is a challenging concept for singers. So in your arias and scenes, ask yourself what do I want to touch? And find a gesture that expresses that. If you want to throw an entire group of courtiers out of your chamber, draw your arm across from one side to another like you are sweeping them away. That is a very meaningful gesture and everyone will understand it including our friends in the Gods. If you are longing for your lover, you might reach out as if you want touch their face. If you want to say 'No, never!' you might use both hands meeting in middle and swiping them apart as if you clear that idea in front of you completely away. The possibilities are endless but make sure you want to touch something. A person, a group, an idea, the past, the future, the money, the lost child. Touch it symbolically with a meaningful gesture.

Gesture exercise:

Close your eyes and I want you to imagine a small kitten is hiding in a cardboard box about 8 feet away from you. She's a very shy kitten and is crying. She pokes her head out of the box and looks at you. You have some food for her so you are trying to coax her over to you to try some of the kitten food. She's considering it but she's not sure so you really have to work at getting her to trust you to walk over. Call her. Entice her. Charm her and encourage her.

Now open your eyes and do exactly what you did before. Call her, entice her, charm her, reassure her.

There is every chance you are using your arms and hands to beckon her over to you. You are trying to draw her to you with a kind of magic invisible string with your hands. And you are making a meaningful gesture based on your desire to touch that kitten.

Another scenario:

Close you eyes and imagine you are standing on a street corner. You look down on end of the street and you see a group of school children crossing the road with their teacher. They are taking their time and the teacher is bit distracted by two of the children who are acting up. Now you look the other way as you hear the noise of a large bus barreling down the road towards the children. The teacher doesn't see the bus and there are still at least 10 children making their way across this broad street. They are some distance away from you so you have time to try to warn the teacher and the children. You can shout, you can do whatever you need to do to get their attention.

Now open your eyes and go through the same scenario in you mind. See those little children in your imagination. How many? What does the teacher look like? Now you see the bus, and it is really moving at a dangerous speed towards the children, a terrible tragedy could take place unless you get the teacher's and the children's attention to move out of the way.

What have your arms and hands been doing? Have they been waving? Have they been shooing the children away off the street? Have they been up trying to get the bus to stop? If so, you have been making very meaningful gestures.

*And did you make parallel gestures or were you able to make asymmetrical gestures? This could take practice and is the skill of a true professional. See below.

Advanced concept

A THOUGHT leads to an ACTION…

Thought leads to an Action -- and possibly a gesture and/or the use of a prop?

Advanced Gesture concepts

- Avoid parallel gestures (when both arms are doing exactly the same thing at the same time mirroring each other) which tend to be unimaginative and look amateurish. Let one arm lead and the other follow. If you are going to gesture with both arms (and by all means you may only use only one arm) but if you use both then let one arm be the leading arm and one the shadowing arm. Put yourself in 3-D.

I once witnessed a four hour Verdi opera where the tenor (who sang wonderfully) spent his entire visual performance making the same parallel gesture over and over again raising his arms up and down like one of those toys where you pull a string and the arms of the little soldier go up together simultaneously. It was so hard to watch. Just a few words and a slight adjustment could have made a huge difference to his performance.

- Use the width of the stage for gestures and movement. Again it's about putting your body in 3 dimensions. If you only gesture US or DS, it won't 'read' to the audience very well. Gestures with width read!

- When gesturing, (rule of thumb) you could bring your arm down at the end of a phrase. Or you could keep your arm up. But what goes up must come down so make a decision on when that will be.

The Stage is divided into 9 squares

Back wall of Stage

USR Up Stage Right	USC Up Stage Centre	USL Up Stage Left
CSR Centre Stage Right	CS Centre Stage	CSL Centre Stage Left
DSR Down Stage Right	DSC Down Stage Centre	DSL Down Stage Left

Audience

Down Stage is nearest the audience and Up Stage is furthest away from the audience. Once you've mastered the names of each square you can write down your moves in shorthand.

C = Centre Stage   UL = Upstage Left
CR = Centre Right   DC = Downstage Centre

CL =Centre Left   DR = Downstage Right
UC = Upstage Centre   DL = Downstage Left
UR = Upstage Right

X = Cross or travelling from one place on the stage to
another.

You can write down your stage directions. Violetta
enters: Upstage Right, she crosses to the table
Downstage Left and sits. She stands, crosses
Downstage Right and exits.

This would look like. Enter UR. X DL to table sit. X DR
exit.

These set moves discovered in the rehearsal are called
Blocking or sometimes called Staging. Once a scene is
'blocked', it is set but of course the blocking can be
changed at any time if need be.

Every actor worth his salt knows the stage is divided into
the Nine Squares and yet it is rarely taught to opera
singers. It such an easy way for the director to tell you
where to go and for you to write down your moves, the
blocking, very quickly and easily.

Writing down your blocking exercise:

We need a director, a stage manager and a singer. The
director tells the singer where to move on the stage using
the 9 Squares, the singer follows the director's
instructions and the stage manager writes them down.
Now another singer, using the stage manager's blocking
shorthand notes, duplicates the moves on the stage.

Practicalities and terminology:

- A skilled actor/singer knows that from the audience's point of view, the stage in an opera house can look very flat. Almost like a painting in a frame. Work out how to put your body comfortably and naturally in 3 dimensions as much as you can. For instance avoid standing face front to the audience. This looks very flat and very 2 dimensional. And it looks rather amateurish Stand slightly asymmetrically. One foot slightly ahead of the other. Stand slightly on the diagonal. Makes you so much more interesting to look at. Worth learning to do this out of habit.

- Gesture with your US arm so you are sharing with the audience and not blocking yourself.

- Step out with your US foot so you're body is open as you first move.

- Write down your stage directions based on the Nine Squares.

- What is a raked stage? A raked stage is a stage that is tilted towards the audience to improve sight lines. Most opera stages are raked.

- Standing at ¼ ½ ¾, R or L. Imagine you are standing Centre Stage. Start at facing full front DC. Now turn slightly and face DR. You are standing at ¼ Right. Now stand and face RC. You are facing ½ Right. Now face UR. You are standing ¾ Right. And if you face directly US you are facing Upstage. This is another fantastic tool for writing down stage directions very efficiently.

Adding to Violetta's blocking: Violetta enters Upstage Right, she crosses to the table Downstage Left and sits facing on a diagonal to the right over the audience. She stands, crosses Downstage Right and exit.

This would look like. Enter UR. X DL to table sit ¼ R X DR exit.

- Understand the terminology of the typical opera stage.

The proscenium arch is the frame of the stage. Can be quite elaborate in European opera houses. The apron is an additional area of stage added in front of the edge of the stage to allow for more playing space.

- Cheating and sharing. Cheating is a term to describe when you place yourself in a way that helps the audience see what is going on. In real life we might not stand this way but as we are professional communicators we know instinctively that we need to make adjustments to accommodate the audience.

When a couple sing a duet where one sings, then another sings, then they both sing, a good colleague will not stare out over the audience while their partner is singing. It's distracting the audience from the person singing. They will give them focus and look towards them. Then when it is their turn to sing they will take it out over the audience and sing while their partner gives them the focus. Then singing together they will look out over the big Imax screen of their imaginations together. This is called Cheating and Sharing.

- Upstaging. This is when you distract from the storytelling and take the focus when you should not. It's not professional and should be avoided.

- Cross in a arc-like way when you can. Crossing in a straight line will look very 2 dimensional, very flat from the audience's point of view. As much as you can, put yourself in 3 dimensions. When you cross the stage, cross in an arc or semicircle. I guarantee you the audience will not notice but they will see much more of you and your body. This is the skill of a true professional.

- How to get out of a chair keeping your back straight keeping your bolero down. From a sitting position, slide the foot which is going to be doing the heavy lifting (i.e. you) under the chair and the other slightly ahead of you and then as you rise press down with that foot under the chair and gently shift your weight onto your front foot. This way you can keep your back straight, bolero down and look elegant as you stand. In a period opera like for instance _Eugen Onegin_, these characters don't schlumpf out of their chairs when they stand. They stand elegantly and effortlessly. And remember when you stand the skill isn't just in doing it elegantly but also doing it in character.

And when you sit the opposite happens. You touch the back of your legs to the edge of the seat, gently slide your foot under the chair and sit transferring the weight to that foot while keeping your bolero down. In Period work you must maintain good relaxed upright posture. Slouching is a bad habit from the past 40 years.

- Don't short circuit communication by crossing your arms, closing your eyes, putting your arms behind your back or clenching your fists etc. A common fault is to look down towards the edge of the stage when you are singing. Trying to hide in plain sight from the audience. Look up and out over the audience to that great big Imax screen where you project your thoughts, hopes, fears, everything you are thinking. Give out and communicate.

- What is stage business? What do I mean if I say that piece of business doesn't 'read'? Business is generally something to do with a prop. A fan, a letter, a glove etc. If the director says it doesn't 'read' they mean it's not working and you might want to try something else.

- Try not to leave a prop that has fallen on the stage just sitting there if you can pick it up. And if you are the Countess you can indicate to a servant to pick it up. We have our audience in the palm of our hand and they are in a childlike zone. So if you drop a prop and you don't pick it up right away, like children they will start focusing on that prop. As time goes on the only thing they will be watching is that prop wondering if someone is going to do something about it and all your hard work singing away will go for nothing.

Period and Style

"History is a tale of human affairs."

Ask yourself:

• What is the period?

• Did people ever think they are living in a 'Period'? No more than we think we are living in an Historic Period now. The fact is we definitely are living in a remarkable Period of human history with extraordinary events going on around us. But being in the middle of it we don't see it that way. Similarly, during the 18th Century Enlightenment for instance, huge changes were taking place around government, science, politics, literature etc. but I doubt anyone thought, "We are 'Georgians' or we are living in the Age of the Enlightenment. They were, as we are now, poised between the past and what is to come. They did not think of themselves as living in a museum exhibit of a 'Period' any more than we think that of our lives now. When you play a period there are rules and ways of behaving but they were not stylised like a posture in a painting. They were based on living attitudes and beliefs.

- What defines an historic period? Things that will define a period: politics, government, social organisation, hygiene, discoveries, inventions, arts, education, costume and fashion, architecture and the home, painting and sculpture, music and dance, composers, religion and philosophy.

Practicalities of Period movement

- Ladies walking and exiting with a train. When you are walking in a train, particularly a long one, think of the train as part of you and always make sure there is room for it behind you. And as a rule of thumb, don't touch or play with the train. To practice in a exercise, walk in a big figure of 8 in your train on the stage or in a figure of 6 to exit.

- Walking in a crinoline. A crinoline in the 19th century was a large more or less round dress which went over a frame with underskirting. When you walk in a crinoline you must take smaller steps and float. Think of yourself like an airship. For the best example of walking beautifully in one, look at Vivien Leigh in Gone With the Wind. There is a scene where she flies down the steps and she floats. Small steps to float not big long thumping strides which will make the dress sway from side to side like a giant bell. Float and keep the dress still as you walk.

- Walking up steps in a long dress or crinoline. To walk up steps in a either of these as you step up you must see the toe of your shoe very clearly. Elegantly lift the front of the skirts with one or both hands, see your toe extending under the dress and then step up. Every step. Or you might just fall on your face like poor Jennifer Lawrence did at the Oscars.

The Style is in the person.

If you find a photo or a painting that reminds you of your character then imagine them moving. Her posture, her clothing, the articles she uses will all dictate how she moves.

How would she play this mandolin? How would she pick up a glass of wine and sip?

How would he aim a revolver in a duel? How would he pick up a quill and dip it into an inkwell?

Certainly one of the best ways you can help yourself in period work is by having good, *relaxed,* upright posture keeping your shoulders down. It was only in relatively modern times that people slouch the way they do now.

Period Movement Exercises

•   Getting out of a chair. Practice sitting and getting out of a chair while keeping your invisible bolero down and your shoulders relaxed and down.

•   Crossing the stage moving very naturally with good relaxed upright posture while walking in a semi-circle to put your body in three dimensions.

•   Walking with a train in a Figure of 8 never letting your train get crumbled or ruckled. Don't touch the train. The direction you walk dictates where the train goes behind you.

- Now combine walking in a train and sitting. If your train is extended stage right next to your chair you are not going to be able to stand and immediately cross right now are you? You will have to start by crossing Stage Left and then turn in a circle either DS or US and then turn keeping the train following in an orderly arrangement behind you.

- Kneeling with a cape and sword. What if you are wearing a long sword and cape and have to kneel in a scene? If you don't get the hilt of the sword forward making the sword more horizontal to your body it will scrape up along your ribs as you kneel. And you better get that cape out of the way of the sword too.

Connecting the dots.

A THOUGHT leads to an ACTION... ...and on occasion, when it will help the story, character or relationships, an action leads to a gesture and/or the use of a prop!

USE the Galaxy of Your Imagination!

Exercise to bring your imagination into play when you sing.

Choose an aria you know very well. Read out the English text and act it out. Look for the story, for the character, for the relationships. You must know as much as possible about this aria to get the most out of this exercise.

Close your eyes and sing it once. Now sing it again also with your eyes closed and really see what the character sees. Start drawing what you see in your imagination in the air. Use both hands. Draw the trees, draw the palace, draw your enemy's face, your lover's face, the setting and the other characters. See everything in minute detail. Use your entire imagination. Let thoughts come to you. Open up your mind and your heart to your aria.

Now open your eyes and sing the aria again. Bring all those thoughts into play and project them out over the audience as if it is a giant Imax screen.

Try it again with your eyes closed. Knit your imagination and your singing and aria together and bring it all to life.

Remember you are only limited by your unlimited imagination!

Advanced Exercise with singing

Step 1: Sing a page or two of music with an action.

(Example: Quando M'en Vo from Boheme - sing with the actions of To Attack, Threaten, Flatter or Dare. For the sake of the exercise choose an action that doesn't really suit the situation in the aria to make it a little more challenging. Just use the aria as a template for the sake of this exercise.)

Step 2: Move in a Figure of Eight singing the aria with the action.

Step 3: Move in a Figure of Eight singing the aria with the action wearing a train.

Step 4: Move in a Figure of Eight singing the aria with the action wearing a train and using a fan or another prop.

Step 5: Move in a Figure of Eight singing the aria with the action wearing a train and using a fan or another prop and sit in a chair correctly.

Putting it all together: Your General Rule of Thumb Approach

• Rehearsal: The word for rehearsal In French is Repetition, in German the word is Probe. You have to do both. Exploring while saving and refining the best of what you find. Over and over again. This is what happens in an opera rehearsal.

• Understand the story

• Understand your character

• Work out and show the relationships

• Show us, don't tell us

• Use actions to get what you want

• Apply your Stage Skills

Never forget our Three Friends in the Gods. Integrate and express the storytelling, the character and their relationships into the music VISUALLY.

A Few Final Thoughts

Regietheater - Director's Theatre

This approach to opera started in Germany for historical reasons. It is very concept-driven, avant garde and can be controversial. Whatever the singer's personal thoughts about Regietheater (or any other production style for that matter) may be, if they accept a contract to perform in an opera, it is not their job to judge the production. Their professional obligation and responsibility is to completely support the concept and do everything in their power as artists and company members to make sure the performance is a success. You will not be doing your best work if do otherwise.

33

Professionalism and being a Good Colleague

There's a phrase one hears with opera singers I like very much. Such and such singer is a 'Good Colleague'. By that they mean, they are always prepared, they are always on time, they never ever compete with another company member, they are kind and supportive and great listeners. They do their very best to foster friendship and camaraderie in the company. They go out of their way to help their fellow singers during rehearsal and during the performance. It's the best compliment one singer can give another. You don't always see it but when you do it stands out a mile. Be a Good Colleague.

And timekeeping. Being on time is a huge part of being a Good Colleague. In most professional opera rehearsals, arriving 5 minutes before the call would be considered late. Arrive at least 15 minutes ahead of time, all personal items stowed and sorted, score open on one side of the room, warmed up physically and vocally and ready to get stuck in. If everyone is there and ready you can even start a little bit early which is a gift to the director and s/he will be very happy about that. The rehearsal period for most professional operas can be remarkably brief. Every minute counts.

And speaking of good colleagues, a singer told me a story of her debut at the Royal Opera House in London in which the wonderful mezzo Joyce DiDonato was singing the central role. Despite it being the first night of a very demanding role in a world class opera company with all the pressure involved, Miss DiDonato sought her out to hug her and wish her well on her ROH debut. I'm sure many singers have similar stories about this generous and lovely lady who is the epitome a good colleague.

Nerves

I saw a blog clip with advice about nerves by Miss DiDonato in which she said for her the best way to manage nerves is to be completely prepared for the role. That is terrific advice of course. Knowing thoroughly what you are doing provides a lot of security. The other thing you can do is focus on the job at hand. Take your mind off yourself and focus on the performance 100%. If you focus on the delivery of the singing, the story, being the character and playing the relationships on the stage, you will not have time to think about yourself and your nerves. Focus on the job. Be aria conscious not self conscious.

34

Some words of wisdom.

My wonderful teacher Rudi Shelly constantly reminded us, "Don't work so hard!" I think he meant that acting is basically a mental process not a forced and physically tense one. He said if you are sweating you are doing it wrong. If you get the right clear and strong thoughts with a good relaxed upright posture, everything else will follow gently and easily. Trying to compensate for a the lack of a strong and powerful thought by physical tension and forcing is just too much hard work. So 'Don't work so hard!'

35

The Vocation of Good Craftsmanship

What is Good Craftsmanship?

This is a golden nugget to leave you with. Focus on how you are doing something, not what you are doing. Focus on honing your skills and craft. Not what you are singing. You may be very lucky and find that you are a very popular Musetta in La Boheme and get to sing it in several productions more than once during the year. If you approach each rehearsal and each performance with the goal of giving the best, the finest performance of this role every single time you will never tire of Musetta. Set goals and standards of craftsmanship which you want to achieve every time you sing this role. Once you have achieved those standards then set even higher ones. Keep striving on your constant progression of improvement.

I once read a remarkable story about the great American actor Alfred Lunt in The Visit by Swiss playwright Friedrich Dürrenmatt. The director Peter Brook came back to see a performance after it had been playing for many months. He went backstage to Mr. Lunt's dressing room for a chat and while they were talking, the actor kept playing he had a stone in his shoe. Finally Peter Brook asked him what he was doing and Alfred Lunt said, 'You know in the scene where I sit down exhausted and take the pebble out of my shoe, should I take out one or two?' He'd been doing the play 8 times a week for months and he was still honing his performance with very fine details. Now that is Good Craftsmanship!! Always focus on how you are doing something and not what you are doing. If you do this, your performance will be consistent, will continuously improve, it will never get stale. And you will never be bored.

List of Exercises

Telling a Story - Little Red Riding-Hood
Androcles and the Lion
Storytelling as a Team
Introduction and Storytelling exercise
Actions Exercise
Conflict Improvisation Exercise
Relationship Exercise
Storytelling and Relationship Exercise - Manon Lescaut
Getting the Thought and the Lemon Exercise
New Idea Exercise

Hiding the Evidence Advanced Acting Exercise
Pull down your Bolero
Meaningful Gesture Exercise
Blocking and Stage Moves Exercise
Period Movement Exercises
Singing with your Imagination Exercise
Advanced Singing Exercise with Costumes and Props

About Norman Cooley

Norman has been involved in the area of performance for over 45 years. He has a B.A. in Theatre from the University of California at Los Angeles (1975-79) and trained as an actor at the Bristol Old Vic Theatre School (1980-82) and worked professionally as an actor for over 22 years.

He has trained hundreds of singers in workshops, in private lessons, at the the *Wales International Academy of Voice*, the *Trinity Laban Conservatoire, Royal Northern College of Music* and by coaching opera companies. He saw his first opera at the age of 12 and the following year performed and sang in four operas professionally.

As an actor, he worked in the West End of London, in repertory throughout the UK and Europe as well as television work and countless advertisements in the UK and Europe. His theatre direction training was at UCLA with Michael Gordon, a noted American theatre and film director and at the Bristol Old Vic Theatre School, he trained as an actor with perhaps the greatest acting teacher of all time, the legendary Rudi Shelly. His training is a combination of Rudi's teachings adapted for the opera house, as well as the work of many other fine teachers including the brilliant Michael Gordon and the excellent Lenore DeKoven.

Norman believes acting in opera should be completely integrated with the singing and support and empower the work of the singer, and should never hamper nor harm good singing technique. It should be as effortless as possible to provide a safe harbour for the singer to sing at their best while creating a fully satisfying performance.

ACTING FOR OPERA
www.actingforopera.co.uk

19823680R00053

Printed in Poland
by Amazon Fulfillment
Poland Sp. z o.o., Wrocław